CLOSER LOOK AT
FORESTS

Cally Hall

COPPER BEECH BOOKS
Brookfield, Connecticut

© Aladdin Books Ltd 1998
Designed and produced by
Aladdin Books Ltd
28 Percy Street
London W1P 0LD

First published in the United States
in 1999 by
Copper Beech Books,
an imprint of
The Millbrook Press
2 Old New Milford Road
Brookfield, Connecticut 06804

Editor
Michael Flaherty

Designer
Jeff Gurney

Picture Research
Brooks Krikler Research

Front cover illustration
Gary Edgar-Hyde

Illustrators
Mike Saunders, Simon Tegg,
Ron Hayward Associates, Gary Hincks,
Ian Moores, Richard Orr, Philip Weare,
David Burroughs, James McDonald,
Louise Nevet

Certain illustrations have appeared in
earlier books created by Aladdin Books.

Consultant
Joyce Pope

Cataloging-in-Publication data is on file at the Library
of Congress.

ISBN 0-7613-0901-2 (lib. bdg.)

5 4 3 2 1

CONTENTS

INTRODUCTION

Forests are large areas that are covered with trees. They are essential to life on earth. Trees help to regulate our atmosphere — without trees we would not have enough oxygen to breathe. Forests provide a home to millions of plants and animals. More than half of all known species are found in rain forests. Throughout the ages, people have used forests for the shelter of trees, their fruits, and their wood for building and fuel. Other forest plants also provide food, dyes, and medicines. Today, forests are still being destroyed — cut down or burned — at a rapid rate.

The types of forest that grow depend on climate, from the cold northern forests to the hot, moist tropical rain forests. In addition to the great bands of forest (see map below), smaller forests develop where the local climate is right. Such local forests include mountain forests, coastal forests, and dry tropical forests.

Too hot, too dry

Forests cannot develop in areas that are too hot or too dry for trees to grow. In hot deserts (above), which receive little or no rainfall, only palm trees survive at oases, where there is enough water.

Too cold

There are no trees — except for tiny willows only 2 inches (5 cm) high — in the polar regions or on high mountains (below) because it is too cold and the fresh water is often frozen.

FORESTS OF

FOREST DISTRIBUTION

Trees need light, water, warmth, and nutrients from the soil to grow. Forests can only develop where these conditions are found in sufficient quantities. Tropical rain forests thrive in the regions along the equator, where the temperature averages 82°F (28°C), and it rains most days. Temperate forests have distinct seasons with cold winters and warm summers. In the colder areas of northern Europe, Asia, and North America, the boreal forests have long, extremely cold winters and short summers (see map right).

North America

South America

Local climatic conditions such as altitude, coastal weather, rainfall, and warm winds affect the development of forests.

ON CLOSER INSPECTION – *Mangrove swamps*

The mangrove swamps, found along tropical shores, are saltwater forests. Mangrove trees (right) are the only trees that can live in salty water. They have roots that extend from their branches into the muddy waters. These help to take up oxygen and to anchor them.

THE WORLD

Enjoyment value
Forests are not only of great economic and environmental value, they are also of important recreational value (below). In many countries, huge areas of forest have been set aside for wildlife conservation. These areas also allow people the space and environment for such activities as hiking, camping, hunting, nature-watching, or just for relaxing and enjoying the natural beauty.

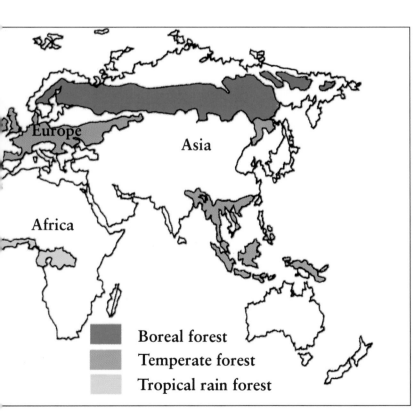

Europe

Asia

Africa

Boreal forest
Temperate forest
Tropical rain forest

For example, conditions similar to those needed for boreal (northern) forests to grow are also found high on the slopes of some mountains.

Temperate forests used to cover vast areas of North America, Europe, and Asia. Most temperate regions have warm summers and short winters. The soil is fertile and rain is plentiful. These are also good conditions for growing crops and rearing livestock, so much of these ancient forests has been cleared and the land used for farming.

TEMPERATE

Brambles

Brambles (above), such as blackberries and loganberries, grow in temperate areas. When land has been cleared, brambles often grow before trees become reestablished.

Within five years, land is covered with undergrowth and brambles.

Land previously cleared of deciduous broadleaved trees.

After twenty-five years, young broad-leaved trees cover the land again.

DECIDUOUS TREES

The trees of temperate forests are broad-leaved, having flat, veined leaves. Most of these temperate forest trees are deciduous — they shed their leaves in fall. The trees survive the winter in a dormant (sleeping) state and grow new leaf buds in the spring.

The development of deciduous forests (left) has been studied by watching the regrowth of cleared land. Thistles, willow herb, and other weeds grow first. They are followed by brambles and ferns, such as bracken, and then larger shrubs and saplings (young trees).

FORESTS

ICE AGE

During the last ice age, which ended about ten thousand years ago, glaciers and ice sheets reached as far south as the Great Lakes and covered much of northern Europe (below). As the ice advanced from the north, the areas covered by temperate forest moved farther south until the ice receded.

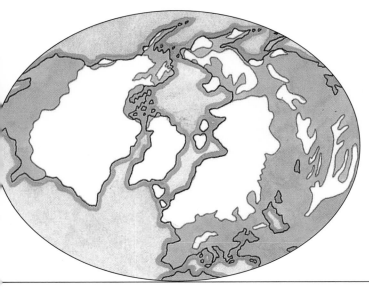

TREE SQUIRRELS

Temperate forests are rich in animal life, such as foxes, badgers, and squirrels (above). Red and gray squirrels are well adapted to forest life. They are agile, both on the ground and in the trees. They feed on a wide range of nuts, berries, fruits, seeds, and fungi, and hide food for the winter. Squirrels build weatherproof nests, called dreys, from twigs and leaves in the branches, or they find shelter in hollow trunks.

he varied plants of the temperate forest grow to different heights. Taller trees, such as the oak, maple, and ash, receive the heat and light of the sun and cast shade over smaller trees and plants. On the forest floor, the moisture and shade allow fungi, lichen, and mosses to thrive.

THE FOREST

Bracken
The herb layer of a temperate forest is made up of soft-stemmed plants such as ferns, grasses, and wild flowers. A species of fern, called bracken (above), is widespread across the world. It likes damp shady areas and is common in temperate woodland when the soil is acidic.

TALL TREES
All forests are made up of horizontal layers, or stories, from the tallest trees down to the lichens and mosses on the forest floor. The branches and leaves of the tallest trees form the top layer, or canopy. In temperate forests the canopy is formed by such tall trees as the oak, beech, sycamore, and in drier areas, silver birch (below). Beneath these, in the understory, are smaller trees such as the holly and hazel, which survive in the shade of the canopy.

Canopy

Oak   Silver birch   Horse chestnut   Beech   Sycamore

Mistletoe (right) is a green plant that grows on tree branches in temperate and tropical regions. The sticky seeds are spread by birds. Once they attach to a tree, the mistletoe's roots grow through the bark to tap the tree's sap.

IN LAYERS

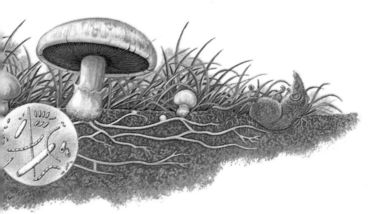

FUNGI AND BACTERIA

The soils of the temperate forests and woodlands are generally fertile, brown soils. Leaves that drop from the trees in the fall add to the twigs, animal droppings, and dead animals and plants scattered on the forest floor. This layer is broken down by organisms such as insects, fungi, and bacteria (above) into chemical compounds that are plowed into the soil by burrowing worms and other animals for new plant growth.

Cool and damp

Lichens, mosses, and liverworts (right) flourish in the cool damp of the forest floor. They also cover rocks and grow on tree trunks. Mosses and liverworts don't have real roots and take in much of their water through their leaves. Lichens consist of fungi and algae living together. They can also survive in drier, colder climates.

The seasonal cycle through spring, summer, fall, and winter gives the temperate forest its distinctive features. In spring there is the growth of ground-living flowers before the full burst of summer cover. The leaves then take on the reds, yellows, and browns of fall, before being shed for the winter.

CYCLING

Birds in spring
In spring, birds, such as the common jay (above), find a mate and use the materials of the forest, such as twigs, leaves, and dried grasses, to make nests in which to lay their eggs. When the eggs hatch, many birds feed the chicks insects, which also hatch in great numbers in spring.

THE CHANGING FACE OF THE FOREST

During the warm summer the thick canopy of leaves (below left) blocks sunlight from much of the ground. The trees provide cover for animals such as hedgehogs, rabbits, foxes, badgers, and deer. Thousands of insects feast on the plants and, in turn, are eaten by birds. In the fall, leaves change color before they are shed (below middle). As winter approaches, many birds fly south to warmer climates. Most trees and bushes seem lifeless, having shed all their leaves (below right). As the snow arrives, many animals must still venture out in search of food.

Winter

Summer

Fall

On Closer Inspection
– *Woodland flowers*

Many woodland flowers, such as violets and trillium in the United States and bluebells in England, flower in spring. They take advantage of the sunlight that reaches the forest floor before it is cut off by new leaves on the trees.

SEASONS

Blooming spring

In temperate forests during the spring, trees and other plants begin to flower. Most of the tree species in these forests, such as oak, ash, elm, and beech, are pollinated by the wind. Other species, such as horse chestnut and many of the plants in the herb layer, produce colorful or large flowers to attract insects, which carry pollen from flower to flower (below).

THE BIG SLEEP

To avoid the cold weather and the lack of food that winter brings, some mammals, such as bats and hedgehogs (above), hide away and go into a sleep called hibernation. During hibernation their temperature drops, and their heartbeat and all their body functions slow down. They live off fat reserves during this winter sleep.

oreal forests, also called taiga, are the coldest and driest forests of the world. The word *boreal* means *northern*. They cover cold northern regions of the world (below). These forests have long, freezing winters and a short growing period in the brief summers. The majority of trees in boreal forests have needle-shaped leaves, which they keep throughout the winter.

BOREAL

Forest dwellers
Many species of deer are boreal forest dwellers (above). They eat shoots, leaves, and grasses, feeding mainly at dawn and dusk, and often staying near the forest's edge. They can outrun most predators, such as wolves and bears, but often prefer to stay motionless, relying on the forest to give them cover until a predator has passed.

About 17 percent of the earth's total landmass is covered with boreal forest.

DISTRIBUTION OF BOREAL FORESTS

The broad band of conifers (cone-bearing trees) that circles the world (below), running through Alaska and Canada, northern Europe, and northern Asia, makes up the earth's boreal forests. It includes the largest uninterrupted area of forest on earth — the Siberian taiga — which stretches from Norway in the west to Kamchatka in the east.

Norway

Kamchatka

Land

17% boreal

ON CLOSER INSPECTION
– *Christmas trees*

Bringing a conifer into the house at Christmas and decorating it is a medieval German tradition. The first Christmas trees arrived in the United States with German settlers in the early 1800s. Today the Norwegian spruce is the most popular Christmas tree.

FORESTS

BOREAL PREDATORS

The northern forests are home to fewer animal species than their warmer counterparts. But they still support enough game to feed their own range of meat-eaters, from pine martens and minks to wolves and bears (below), and even the Siberian tiger, the largest cat in the world.

Scots pine

White spruce

Balsam fir

Larch

Fraction of other species in a boreal forest

Fraction of conifers in a boreal forest

TREE TYPES

Boreal forests contain a smaller number of tree species than other types of forest. These species are nearly all cone-bearing trees, or conifers. Spruce, fir, pine, and larch are the most common. Where temperatures are higher, such as at the edge of lakes and in river valleys, some broad-leaved trees also grow. These include the deciduous willows, birches, and poplars.

A lmost all conifers are evergreen trees — they do not lose all their leaves in winter, but keep them all year round. The small, tough leaves are lost and replaced gradually over several years, so there are always enough for the tree to remain looking green throughout the year.

CONES AND

Snowy pines

Coniferous trees are adapted to severe winters. Their cone shape prevents most of the snow from settling on the branches, so they don't crack under the weight. The supple wood bends easily in high winds. This shape also allows the weak winter sunlight to reach every tree. Any heat reflected from the snow-covered ground is trapped beneath the branches (below). Conifers have shallow roots that spread out to collect surface water.

Sunlight

Heat

Needles

Most conifers have short, narrow leaves called needles. They have a small surface area and a coating of wax. This keeps water loss from the leaves to a minimum and helps to shed snow. A natural antifreeze within the needles helps prevent them from freezing in winter.

A seed falls to earth.

The plumule is green.

The radical grows into the soil.

SEEDLINGS

Seeds that have found a place with enough light and water will be able to germinate (sprout). The seed begins to take up water. It swells and the covering (case) cracks. The new seedling sends a root, or radical, into the soil and a green shoot, or plumule, grows up toward the light.

As the seed's leaves unfold, they may push the seed case off (above)

NEEDLES

CONES

Most conifers have male and female cones on the same tree. Male cones produce pollen and female cones carry ovules, or unfertilized seeds, between their scales. The pollen is blown by the wind to fertilize the ovules. The ovules then grow into seeds. The female cones mature and open to release the seeds, which are dispersed by the wind.

Cone scales

Uncovered seeds

Female cones dry and open to release their seeds.

Male cones

Naked seeds
Conifers belong to the group called gymnosperms, meaning open or uncovered seeds. Conifer seeds lie naked in their cones (above).

An immature female cone containing ovules

A fertilized female cone grows and matures.

Two main types of forest occur in the tropics — seasonal forests and rain forests. Seasonal forests grow where there are definite rainy and dry seasons. Many of the trees are deciduous, shedding their leaves in the dry season. Rain forests grow where it is warm and wet all year around. Most of the trees are broad-leaved evergreens, such as nutmeg.

TROPICAL

Strangler figs
The strangler fig starts growing in the branches of a tree. It sends roots down to the soil. As more roots take hold, the tree is gradually enclosed and may eventually die (above).

Epiphyte
Epiphytes such as this bromeliad (below) are plants that live on other plants without harming them or taking anything from them. They live off rainwater and nutrients in rotting leaves.

Equator

TROPICAL
RAIN FOREST ZONES
The tropics form a wide band around the equator. Tropical rain forests grow in regions of South and Central America, western Africa, Southeast Asia, and parts of Australasia (above). These regions experience temperatures from 68° to 95°F (20° to 35°C) and about 80 inches (200 cm) of rainfall per year. The forest air is always humid. Dense plant growth can be found wherever sunlight falls. The largest tropical rain forest is found in South America.

ON CLOSER INSPECTION
– *Added support*

The taller trees of the tropical forest grow thick buttresses up to 30 feet (10 m) high. The buttresses are triangular wedges (right) of hardwood that radiate out from the trunk. They help support these giant trees, which have shallow roots.

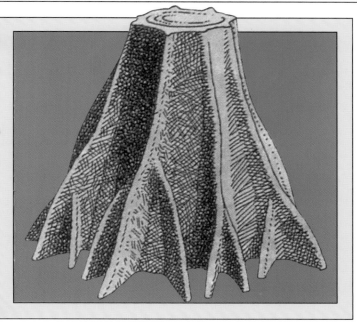

FORESTS

Emergent tree

Uppermost canopy

REACHING FOR THE LIGHT

The rain forest has between three and five stories, or canopies. The uppermost canopy is about 130 feet (40 m) high and receives most of the sunlight. Some trees, called emergents, grow taller than this, often as high as 200 feet (60 m). Each story has its characteristic trees, climbing plants, and epiphytes. Little light reaches the forest floor. Few shrubs and herbs can survive in such shade, so the undergrowth is usually sparse.

Toucan

Hornbill

Look-alikes

Toucans and hornbills (above) each have large beaks that are well-adapted for a diet of nuts and fruit. But they are not related. Toucans live in the forests of South America, while hornbills are found in the forests of Africa and Asia.

As a result of the climate, tropical rain forests have the most varied plant and animal life of any habitat. Conditions vary at different levels in these forests. Some animals confine themselves to a particular level, high up in the canopy or down on the forest floor. Others, such as monkeys, can move more freely between levels.

FROM TOP

GROUND DWELLERS

Many ground-dwelling animals of the rain forest, such as the royal antelope (10 inches (25 cm) high at the shoulder), are smaller than their counterparts living in more open surroundings. But some seem to have become relative giants. The capybara (above) is a shy ground-dweller, and is in fact the world's largest rodent (up to 1.5 feet (50 cm) at the shoulder and over 100 pounds (45 kg)).

FOREST RECYCLERS

The floor of the rain forest is dark and damp — ideal conditions for the forest recyclers, the creatures that return plant and animal matter to the soil. As with the temperate forests, these include insects, spiders, snails, worms, fungi, and bacteria (see page 11). Unlike the nutrient-rich temperate forest soil, the rain forest soil gives up its nutrients almost as soon as it receives them. The trees have shallow roots and are in constant competition to absorb the nutrients near the surface.

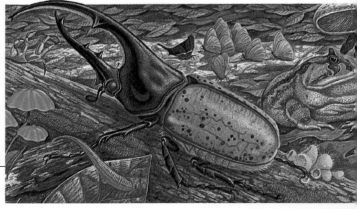

ON CLOSER INSPECTION – *Morpho butterfly*

There are over one hundred thousand species of butterflies and moths. Butterflies are among the most brightly colored insects on earth. The blue morpho butterfly (right) lives in the forests of South America. If the forests disappear, so will these beautiful creatures.

TO BOTTOM

Squirrel monkey

Howler

Macaws

Chimpanzee

Sloth

Leopard

Colobus monkey

Allens opossum

The branches of the canopy and understory are like a highway through the forest for the animals as they search for food.

Four-striped squirrel

Life at the top

The dense branches of the canopies support the greatest number of animal species in the rain forest, because they provide a rich variety of food, from fruits and leaves to insects and birds' eggs. Some birds, such as macaws, and bats eat the plentiful supply of fruit. Monkeys and squirrels make their way swiftly through the branches from one level to another, eating fruits, leaves, and flowers. All must be wary of predators, such as eagles that fly above, and jaguars and snakes that move through the branches.

Forest cures

Forest people have used some forest plants as traditional medicines. Scientists have used their knowledge to develop new drugs from substances extracted from these plants. More than a quarter of the world's most important medicines come from rain forest plants. The diagram below shows three major examples of important medicinal plants. A small purple flower from Madagascar called the rosy periwinkle is used in the treatment of leukemia. Some eye disorders may be treated with medicines from the calabar bean of West Africa. Papaya from Latin America is used to treat stomach complaints.

Humans have always used the fores for materials, food, and medicine The early hunters and gatherers ha little permanent effect on the forests, movin to new hunting grounds regularly and letting the forest regrow. Forest peoples such as the Animarmi Indians of the Amazon still try to live in this way.

LIVING IN

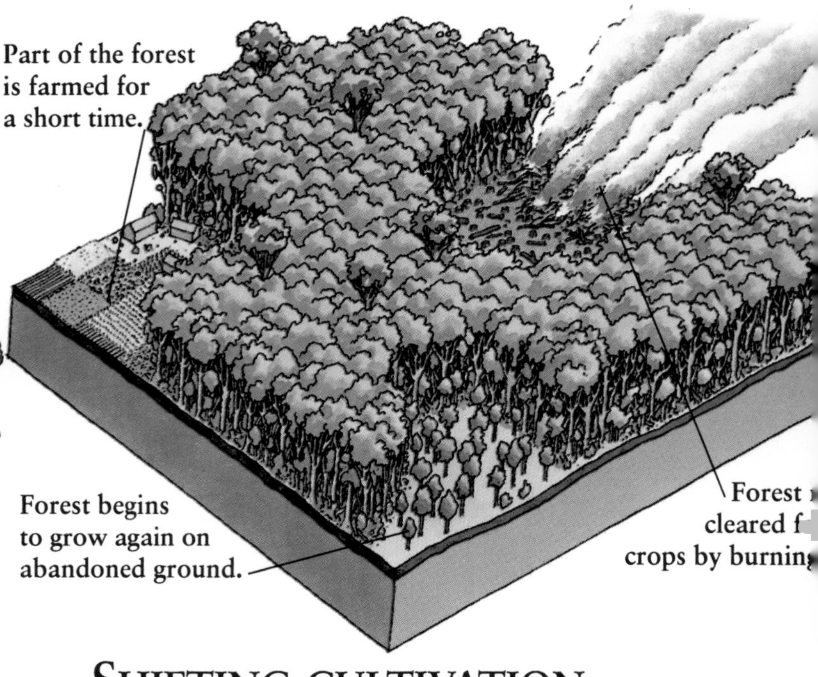

Eye disorders

Leukemia

Stomach illness

Part of the forest is farmed for a short time.

Forest begins to grow again on abandoned ground.

Forest cleared f crops by burnin

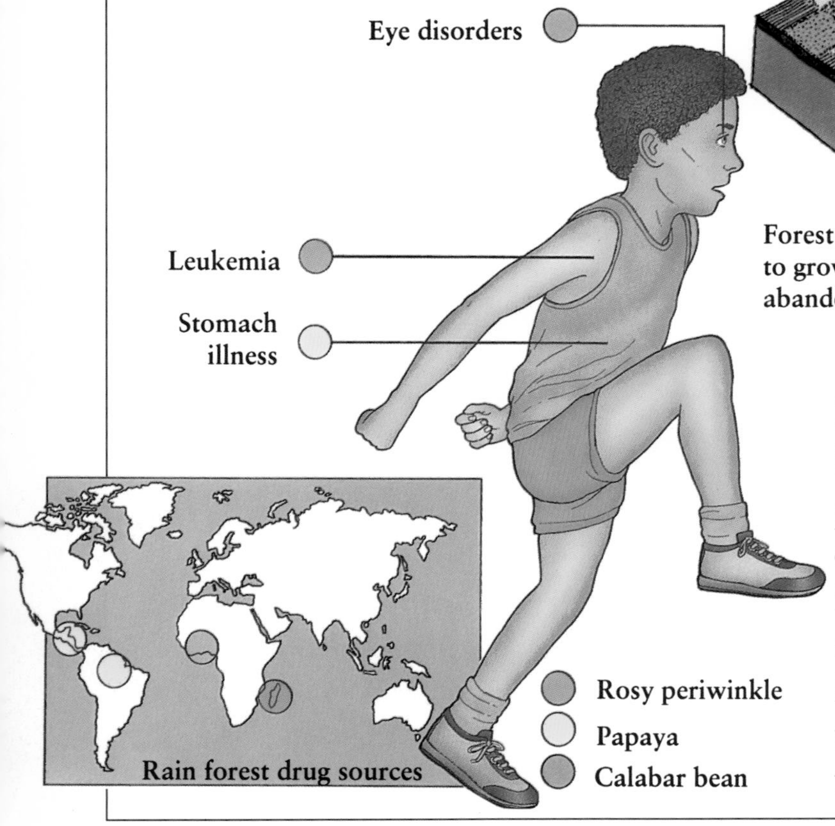

Rosy periwinkle

Papaya

Calabar bean

Rain forest drug sources

SHIFTING CULTIVATION

Some of the peoples of the rain forests practice a kind of farming called shifting cultivation. They burn a small area of forest (above). The ash enriches the soil so that crops can grow. When the soil loses its fertility, the forest people move to a new area. By moving on regularly the forest is given time to recover.

FORESTS

Hunting
Many forest people survive mainly by hunting animals, fishing, and gathering fruit, nuts, and berries. They are called hunter-gatherers. Common hunting methods include setting traps or creeping up slowly on the prey and attacking with arrows, spears, or knives. Some Amazon Indians still hunt with darts and arrows dipped in poisons from the skin secretions of forest frogs (below) or from certain plants.

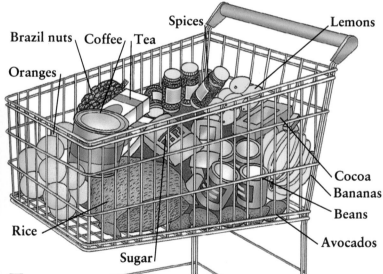

Spices
Lemons
Brazil nuts
Coffee
Tea
Oranges
Cocoa
Bananas
Beans
Rice
Avocados
Sugar

FROM FOREST TO MARKET
A quick look in a supermarket shopping cart (above) will show some of the many common foods, spices, and drinks that originally came from rain forests. Many of these, such as bananas, pineapples, coffee, rice, and tea, are now grown in great quantities in places around the world where the climate is favorable, on large areas of land called plantations.

arth's climate changes, such as the various ice ages, have led to widespread forest destruction and animal extinction. Nowadays, human activity is destroying forests more rapidly than ever before. Trees are felled for timber, burned to clear land, or killed through pollution. This destruction is adding to global warming (see page 25).

FOREST

Acid rain

Pollution from industry and car exhausts in one area can fall as acid rain many miles away. Acid rain destroys forests by killing the trees. The acid destroys important minerals in both the leaves and the soil. The leaves die, and the trees become too weak to resist attack by disease, fungi, or frost. The trees die and the forest is lost (above).

DEFORESTATION

Since the nineteenth century, vast areas of forest have been cleared for timber, fuel, and farming. Forest destruction is called deforestation. Today, tropical rain forests experience severe deforestation. Without the trees, the soil is left unprotected from the rain and wind. Floods become more likely, leading to landslides as rain washes the soil downhill. Disastrous landslides occurred in Italy in 1998, killing many people.

About six thousand years ago, forests still covered most of the land (left). People began to clear forests with stone tools and fire to make way for crops and livestock.

Forest
Land

About two thousand years ago, people had developed metal tools. Forest clearance became easier. Metal working and other new industries also needed more wood as fuel.

Forest
Land

Land
Forest

By two hundred years ago, most of Europe's temperate forests had been chopped down. The same began to happen in North America and Australasia. Today, it is the tropical rain forests.

ON CLOSER INSPECTION
– Animals in danger

Gorillas live in areas of the African rain forest (right). They are easy prey for hunters, who kill them for their skulls or for food. Also, their habitat is disappearing as the trees are cut down. Some are now protected in National Parks.

Rain forest
AFRICA

Home range of gorillas

DESTRUCTION

Carbon dioxide taken in

Water evaporates from the oceans

Moisture taken in

Carbon dioxide given out

Oxygen given out

After deforestation, rain may wash the soil from slopes as there are no longer any tree roots to keep the soil in place.

Lake Kariba

Lake Kariba (below), in Africa, now covers thousands of trees. The building of the Kariba dam caused the river valley before the dam to flood. Now only a few treetops can be seen above water. As these rot they will eventually fall over.

GLOBAL WARMING

Living trees take in carbon dioxide (CO_2) and give out oxygen (O_2), helping to maintain the balance of gases in the atmosphere. When forests are destroyed, there are fewer trees to use the CO_2 and it builds up in the atmosphere. Industry has also increased the amount of CO_2 in the atmosphere. CO_2, along with other gases, acts like a greenhouse, trapping heat in the atmosphere. As the amount of CO_2 increases, more of the sun's heat is trapped. This is called global warming. It may have dangerous effects on the climate.

Forestry
Forestry is the science of forest management. By selecting which trees to plant and which to fell, the forest can provide timber and still be a home for wildlife.

M

odern methods of forest management include the replanting of trees (reforestation) and the planting of trees alongside crops (agroforestry). In Nigeria and Thailand, agroforestry has been introduced in some areas to encourage farmers to plant trees. But replanting land with non-native, fast-growing trees destroys the local animal life, which is tied to the native species of trees and plants.

FOREST

PRUNING
Pollarding (left) used to be an important form of tree pruning. It produces many thin new branches, once used for firewood. Today, tree pruning improves the quality of fruit, and helps prevent transplanted trees from losing too much water.

HARDWOODS
Broad-leaved trees (right), such as maple, teak, and walnut are called hardwoods, while conifers, such as pine, are called softwoods. Many hardwoods, such as teak, come from the rain forests. These trees produce hard-wearing wood. They take a long time to mature, making them very expensive.

On Closer Inspection
– Tree planting

Trees use carbon dioxide (CO_2) from the air to make their food. This process helps prevent carbon dioxide from building up in the atmosphere and helps reduce global warming (see page 25). The planting of more trees will benefit the environment and future generations.

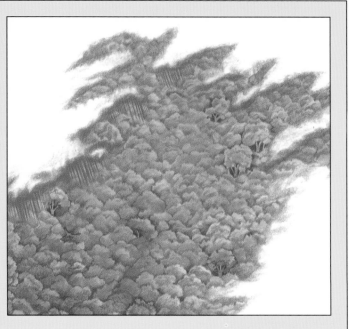

MANAGEMENT

REFORESTATION

Some areas in Brazil that have been cleared of their native forest are being replanted with fast-growing trees such as eucalyptus, which can be harvested after twenty years. This is to encourage local people to replant trees because it is profitable for them to do so.

PAPER

With increased awareness of the environmental issues surrounding deforestation, the idea of recycling paper and paper products has become commonplace. With improvements in technology, better quality recycled paper can be manufactured.

The tree itself is amazing in many ways. Some trees grow over 330 feet (100 m) tall with only a trunk and roots to support them. Trees take in water and nutrients from the soil and can transport them right up to their highest branches and farthest leaves. Trees also support many other living things, providing them with food and shelter.

THE TREE

Tree rings
The number of rings inside the trunk of a temperate tree (above) tell us how old the tree is. The rings' thickness and color also tell us about the weather conditions during the tree's lifetime.

THE OAK TREE
The oak is about 250 years old by the time it is 20 feet (6 m) in girth and may eventually reach 50 feet (15 m). It can grow as tall as 100 feet (30 m). Its fruit is the acorn, a nut that grows in a shallow cup and contains a single seed. The oak tree can support as many as 400 species (right). Birds and squirrels build nests in the branches and the trunk. Insects live in the wood and under the bark. Larger creatures, such as badgers, may build homes among the roots.

ON CLOSER INSPECTION
– Bonsai tree

A bonsai tree (right) is a dwarf tree that has had its growth restricted by careful pruning. Winding wires around the trunk and branches also restricts growth and helps shape the tree. These small, ornamental trees are grown in bowls (bonsai means "bowl cultivation" in Japanese). The art of bonsai originated in China and then spread to Japan.

RATES OF GROWTH

With an idea of how fast different types of tree grow, it is possible to estimate their age. The diagram below compares the height of an oak tree (hardwood) to that of a Scots pine (softwood) with age. The oak is usually felled when it is 100 years old. The Scots pine grows faster than the oak and reaches its full height after 60 years. Today, softwood trees are usually planted at the same rate as they are cut down. This ensures that supply of softwood will never run out.

Tallest and oldest

Among the tallest species of tree in the world is the giant California redwood (right). California redwoods almost 370 feet (113 m) tall have been recorded. The oldest trees in the world are the bristlecone pines (above). The oldest recorded bristlecone pine was 5,100 years old. There is a living bristlecone pine in California called Methuselah that is about 4,700 years old.

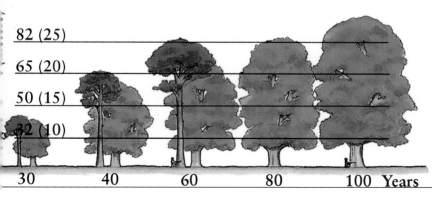

82 (25)
65 (20)
50 (15)
32 (10)

30   40   60   80   100 Years

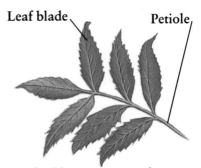

Leaf blade

Petiole

Needlelike pine

Featherlike mountain ash

Hand-shaped sycamore

Macedonian oak with notches around its edge

Fanlike gingko

Handlike horse chestnut

TREE IDENTIFICATION BY LEAF SHAPE

FOREST PROJECTS

KEEPING A DIARY

Choose a tree to study. Look at its trunk, branches, and leaves. Collect leaves, draw a sketch, or make a bark rubbing by laying a piece of paper against the trunk and rubbing the paper with a crayon. Look for birds, mammals, and insects, but try not to disturb them. Study the tree over a year to see how it changes with the seasons.

OAK

Spring — Buds open. Birds start nesting. Some fungus on the trunk.

Summer — Holes in leaves from caterpillars feeding. Baby birds hatched.

Fall — Leaves change color and fall. Acorns on the ground.

Looking at the leaf shape (above) can help to identify a tree. Leaves vary in shape and size, from the sharp needles of conifers to the flat, wide leaves of the broad-leaved trees. Broadleaves may be simple, with a single leaf blade attached to the stalk (petiole) or they may be complex, made up of an odd or even number of leaflets. The edge of the leaf (leaf margin) may be smooth, rounded, or jagged like a saw. A leaf may have a glossy surface or be leathery to the touch.

Measure a tree's girth by wrapping a tape measure around the trunk.

Estimating tree height

With the help of a friend you can estimate the height of a tree (above). Have your friend stand next to the tree. Hold a pencil at arm's length and move away from the tree until the pencil looks the same size as your friend. Estimate how many times taller the tree is than your friend. Multiply your friend's height by this number to find the height of the tree.

Acid rain Rain that has become acidic due to airborne pollution from cars, factories, and power plants. When acid rain falls on rivers, lakes, and forests, it damages and kills fish and trees.

Boreal forest Forest of the cold northern regions. It consists mainly of coniferous trees.

Canopy The top layer of a forest, made up of a dense layer of leaves and branches.

Carbon dioxide One of the main greenhouse gases found in the atmosphere.

Conifers Trees with needlelike leaves that produce cones which contain seeds.

Deciduous trees Trees that shed their leaves in winter and grow new leaves in spring. Most broad-leaved trees are deciduous.

Deforestation The destruction of forests by burning, logging, and flooding.

Emergents The occasional taller trees that tower above the canopy of the rain forest.

Evergreen Trees that do not shed all of their leaves in winter. Although all the leaves may be shed and replaced over several years, the tree remains green all the time. Most conifers and many rain forest plants are evergreens.

Germination The development of a seed into a seedling.

Global warming The gradual warming of the earth possibly as a result of the buildup of greenhouse gases in the atmosphere.

Greenhouse gases Gases that act like a one-way barrier, allowing more of the sun's heat to reach the earth than is allowed to escape back into space. The trapped heat warms the atmosphere of the earth.

Gymnosperms Plants that have unprotected or naked seeds, such as conifers and gingkos.

Habitat The natural home of a living thing.

Hardwood Wood from broad-leaved trees.

Herb layer The layer of plant life in a forest that is close to the ground. The plants include species that grow well in the shade, such as ferns and brambles.

Jungle Dense undergrowth found in tropical forests where sunlight reaches the ground.

GLOSSARY

Ovule The undeveloped seed of a plant found in its flower or cone.

Pollination The transfer of pollen grains, which are male, to the female parts (see ovule) of a flower or cone so that seeds may develop.

Rain forest A forest that grows near or on the equator in places where temperatures and rainfall are constantly high throughout the year.

Shifting cultivation A practice by native forest people who clear and cultivate an area of forest, then move on before the land is exhausted, giving it time to recover.

Softwood Wood from coniferous trees.

Taiga Russian name for the cold boreal forest regions of northern continents.

Understory The layer of a forest beneath the canopy. It contains saplings and trees shorter than those that make up the canopy. The understory grows in partial shade and is not as thick as the canopy.

INDEX

Photo Credits

Abbreviations: t-top, m-middle, b-bottom, r-right, l-left, c-center.

Pages 1, 5, 13t, 23, 26m, 27 & 28 — Roger Vlitos. 2–3, 6 both, 9, 10, 15, 19 & 26b — Frank Spooner Pictures. 7t, 12bl & br — Cally Hall. 7b, 12t &bc, 13m, 14, 16 & 17 — Spectrum Colour Library. 8 — Jeff Gurney. 11 & 21 — Bruce Coleman Collection. 25 — Dan Brooks.